About the book

"Explore the blissful realms of eternal truth. Be prepared to experience enlightenment, transformation, and perpetual awakening!"

Adi Shankaras Sutras are widely regarded as a resource, for those in delving deeper into Hindu philosophy or seeking enlightenment. They are often considered concise and easier to grasp compared to Patanjalis Yoga Sutras making them highly relevant for seekers. A true self-realization book at its best.

These Sutras offer a wealth of insights into the essence of reality, self, and its interconnectedness. They provide guidance on cultivating qualities for achieving self-enlightenment, such as focus, mindfulness, and detachment. Moreover, they encourage us to awaken from our state of ignorance and live authentically in alignment with truth. The path they present is both rewarding – an invitation to personal transformation.

Approaching this knowledge by reading a Sutras at a time proves beneficial. Their logical structure allows comprehension and deepening understanding.

Embrace the wisdom encapsulated within Adi Shankaras Sutras and embark on a journey towards self-realization. Free yourself from the constraints of existence. Explore the blissful realms of eternal truth. Be prepared to experience enlightenment, transformation, and perpetual awakening!

A JOURNEY TOWARDS SELF REALIZATION
ADI SHANKARAS SUTRAS

Cover & Graphic Design
Mattias Långström

A JOURNEY
TOWARDS SELF
REALIZATION
ADI SHANKARAS SUTRAS

✳✳✳

Copyright © Jan Fahleman

Publisher: **BHAGWAN 2023**

***About the author**

Adi Shankaras Sutras are carefully interpreted by the author Jan Fahleman – a master of meditation. He has practiced meditation and yoga asanas for many decades and has also written a best-selling book interpreting Patanjali's Yoga Sutras. He has studied Vedic literature and various spiritual masters since the 1970s.

Sri Adi Shankaras Sutras

Atma Bodha

Self-knowledge

Aparokshanbhuti

Self-realization

Bhaja Govindam

Worship of Govinda

Atma Bodha

Self-knowledge

by

Sri Adi Shankara

Shankaracharya

Translation & comments

Jan Fahleman

Preface

Atma Bodha was written by Adi Shankara probably during the beginning of the 8th century. The text consists of 68 verses and describes the non-dualistic philosophy of Advaita Vedanta. Shri Shankara's philosophy is based on the complete identity of Atman and Brahman. All is Brahman, the unity of Godhead. Atman Bodha can be seen as a summary of Adi Shankara's nondualistic philosophy.

The text is dedicated to his disciple Padmapada.
It is a part of the Prakarana Grantha, which is a collection of scriptures or Upanishads written by teachers or spiritual masters, which should help to increase the understanding of Advaita Vedanta.

During travels in India with his disciples, he often engaged in philosophical discussions with representatives of other philosophies. It was an opportunity to declare Advaita Vedanta.

1. I am composing the ATMA-BODHA, this treatise of
the Knowledge of Atman, or Self-knowledge, to serve the
needs of those who have been purified through austerities
and who are peaceful in heart and calm, who are free from
cravings and desirous of liberation.

*The author is Adi Shankara, probably lived in the late 7th
and early 8th centuries in India. He has authored and commented on many of Hinduism's holiest and most important
scriptures. The basis of his philosophy was non-dualistic
Vedanta which asserts that Brahman and Atman are one
and the same. He died young, at the age of 32.*

2. As the fire is the direct cause for cooking, so without
Knowledge no emancipation can be had. Compared with
all other forms of discipline Knowledge of the Atman is the
one direct means for liberation.

*Knowledge brings purity in body and mind and opens up for
liberation and insight. The presence of Atman (Consciousness) is the means to liberation.*

3. Action cannot destroy ignorance, for it is not in conflict with or opposed to ignorance. Knowledge does verily destroy ignorance as light destroys dense darkness.

4. Atman appears to be finite because of ignorance. When ignorance is destroyed, Atman which does not admit of any multiplicity truly reveals itself by itself: like the Sun when the clouds is removed.

Through ignorance Atman is regarded as limited, but like the sun existing behind the clouds, though the eye cannot see it, the eternal unlimited Atman exists even though one is unaware of it.

5. Through repeated practice of Knowledge purifies the Self ('Jivatman'), stained by ignorance and then disappears itself - as the powder of the 'Kataka-nut' settles down after it has cleansed the muddy water.

Kataka is a nut that, according to Ayurvedic treatment, can purify water.

6. The world which is full of attachments, aversions, etc., is like a dream. It appears to be real, as long as it continues but appears to be unreal when one is awake.

Being present in the mind is often experienced as the only reality. Only when presence in Consciousness reveals the relative unreality, can one realize that one has experienced a dream from which one awakens to true wisdom.

7. The Jagat (the world) appears to be true (Satyam) so long as the non-dual Brahman, the basis of all this creation, is not known. It is like the illusion of silver in an oyster-shell.

8. Like bubbles in the water, the worlds rise, exist and dissolve in the Supreme Self, which is the material cause and the prop of everything.

9. All the manifested world of things and beings are projected by imagination upon the substratum which is the Eternal All-pervading Vishnu, whose nature is Existence-Intelligence; just as the different ornaments are all made out of the same gold.

10. The All-pervading Akasa appears to be diverse on account of its association with various conditionings (Upadhis) which are different from each other. Space becomes one on the destruction of these limiting adjuncts: So also the Omnipresent Truth appears to be diverse on account of Its association with the various Upadhis and becomes one on the destruction of these Upadhis.

The mind is constantly creating experiences (Upadhis) that bind awareness to relative existence (to space, Akasa). Being established in Consciousness, these Upadhis, limitations, can be observed and regarded as false and transitory. They then lose their ability to influence awareness. They do not need to be analyzed or thought about, only observed.

11. Because of Its association with different conditionings (Upadhis) such ideas as caste, colour and position are super-imposed upon the Atman, as flavour, colour, etc., are super-imposed on water.

As long as the mind dominates the awareness, various conditions will assert themselves and bind the attention. The mind always strives to make comparisons and distinguish different phenomena.

12. Determined for each individual by his own past actions
and made up of the five elements – that have gone through
the process of "five-fold selfdivision and mutual combination" (Pancheekarana) – are born the gross-body, the
medium through which pleasure and pain are experienced,
the tent-of-experiences.

*As long as awareness is dependent on the five senses, a physi-
cal body is required for sensory experiences to be established
and experienced.*

13. The five Pranas, the ten organs and the Manas and the
Buddhi, formed from the rudimentary elements (Tanmatras) before their "five-fold division and mutual combination with one another" (Pancheekarana) and this is the
subtle body, the instruments-of-experience (of the individual).

*The subtle body enables experiences on an individual level.
It is made of five pranas, which are five energies that sustain
life energy (prana, apana, samana, vyana and udana), sense
organs, manas (mind) and buddhi (intellect). The rudimentary elements, tanmatras are; smell, taste, touch, sound and
form that enable sensory experiences.*

14. Avidya which is indescribable and beginningless is the Causal Body. Know for certain the Atman is other than these three conditioning bodies (Upadhis).

Ignorance (about the relationship between the mind and Consciousness) is a state of awareness that is linked to the temporary causal body, that Atman, which is unbound and eternal, is not affected by that.

15. In its identification with the five-sheaths the Immaculate Atman appears to have borrowed their qualities upon Itself; as in the case of a crystal which appears to gather unto itself colour of its vicinity (blue cloth, etc.).

Atman is unconditional and without characteristics in itself, but just as a clear diamond may seem blue near a blue fabric, Atman may be perceived to have attribute when the mind have experiences. It's Avidya.

16. Through discriminative self-analysis and logical thinking one should separate the Pure Atman within from the sheaths as one separates the rice from the husk, bran, etc., that are covering it.

By being present in Consciousness, ignorance disappears and the pure Atman appears clearly, while the mind fades away.

17. The Atman does not shine in everything although He is All-pervading. He is manifest only in the inner equipment, the intellect (Buddhi): just as the reflection in a clean mirror.

Just as the sun causes the moon to appear to shine, so Atman causes the intellect (Buddhi) to appear to reflect Atman.

18. One should understand that the Atman is always like the King, distinct from the body, senses, mind and intellect, all of which constitute the matter (Prakriti); and is the witness of their functions.

Atman's relation to Prakriti is a present witness. Atman does not participate in the relative functions. Paradoxically, Atman is also basically the relative existence.

19. The moon appears to be running when the clouds move in the sky. Likewise to the non-discriminating person the Atman appears to be active when It is observed through the functions of the sense-organs.

When a person is only present in the mind and not present in the Atman, one sees the Atman through the relative perspective of the mind.

20. Depending upon the energy of vitality of Consciousness (Atma Chaitanya) the body, senses, mind and intellect engage themselves in their respective activities, just as men work depending upon the light of the Sun.

Consciousness is present in both relative and absolute eternal existence, no dimensions or states of awareness are exempt.

21. Fools, because they lack in their powers of discrimination superimpose on the Atman, the Absolute-Existence-Knowledge (Sat-Chit), all the varied functions of the body and the senses, just as they attribute blue colour and the like to the sky.

Since one cannot distinguish Atman from the mind, one believes that the qualities of the mind also apply to Atman, just as one is deceived into thinking that the sky is blue because it sometimes has qualities that appear to be blue.

22. The tremblings that belong to the waters are attributed through ignorance to the reflected moon dancing on
it: likewise agency of action, of enjoyment and of other
limitations (which really belong to the mind) are delusively
understood as the nature of Atman.

23. Attachment, desire, pleasure, pain, etc., are perceived
to exist so long as Buddhi or mind functions. They are
not perceived in deep sleep when the mind ceases to exist.
Therefore they belong to the mind alone and not to the
Atman.

*During deep sleep there is no conscious presence. In this state
of awareness only the mind exists and not the clear conscious
presence of Atman. During the dream sleep state of awareness, there is conscious presence in various experiences and
sensory sensations that bind awareness to the mind.*

24. Just as luminosity is the nature of the Sun, coolness of
water and heat of fire, so too the nature of the Atman is
Eternity, Purity, Reality, Consciousness and Bliss.

*Being aware in the eternity of Atman can be experienced as;
reality (truth), purity and bliss. In Vedanta, one often speaks
of Sat-Chit-Ananda -Truth-Consciousness-Bliss).*

25. By the indiscriminate blending of the two - the Existence-Knowledgeaspect of the Self and the thought-wave of the intellect - there arises the notion of "I know".

Not being fully established in Atman and thereby gaining intuitive knowledge that is mixed with the musings of the intellect can mean confusion that manifests itself as one thinks one knows.

26. Atman never does anything and the intellect of its own accord has no capacity to experience 'I know'. But the individuality in us delusorily thinks he is himself the seer and the knower.

This is because ignorance creates an illusion when you think that "I know" and that knowledge comes from the intellect.

27. Just as the person who regards a rope as a snake is overcome by fear, so also one considering oneself as the ego (Jiva) is overcome by fear. The egocentric individuality in us regains fearlessness by realising that It is not a Jiva but is Itself the Supreme Soul.

When one realizes that the snake is a rope, fear disappears immediately, just as one becomes fearless when one realizes that Jivan is Atman.

28. Just as a lamp illumines a jar or a pot, so also the Atman illumines the mind and the sense organs, etc. These material-objects by themselves cannot illumine themselves because they are inert.

Atmanis present in everything. Both the mind and the sense organs are supported by Atman. In the same way that some objects in relative existence are active and affect other objects that are inactive.

29. A lighted-lamp does not need another lamp to illumine its light. So too, Atman which is Knowledge itself needs no other knowledge to know it.

30. By a process of negation of the conditionings (Upadhis) through the help of the scriptural statement; 'It is not this, It is not this', the oneness of the individual soul and the Supreme Soul, as indicated by the great Mahavakyas, has to be realised.

One process to approach the truth and go beyond the words and the intellect is to apply "it is not this, it is not this" which is usually called "neti, neti" and is a process that applies negation.

31. The body, etc., up to the "Causal Body" - Ignorance - which are objects perceived, are as perishable as bubbles. Realise through discrimination that I am the 'Pure Brahman' ever completely separate from all these.

The various body systems give rise to impressions of material objects and mental activities that are impermanent like soap bubbles in the sky. He who is consciously present in Consciousness constantly distinguishes relative existence from absolute existence.

32. I am other than the body and so I am free from changes such as birth, wrinkling, senility, death, etc. I have nothing to do with the sense objects such as sound and taste, for I am without the sense-organs.

Not being bound to the relative existence is the result of the distinguishing process.

33. I am other than the mind and hence, I am free from sorrow, attachment, malice and fear, for "HE is without breath and without mind, Pure, etc.", is the Commandment of the great scripture, the Upanishads.

Consciousness is independent and therefore without breath and mind. The Upanishads are scriptures that document the relationship between Brahman, Atman and Jivan.

34. I am without attributes and actions; Eternal (Nitya) without any desire and thought (Nirvikalpa), without any dirt (Niranjana), without any change (Nirvikara), without form (Nirakara), ever-liberated (Nitya Mukta) ever-pure (Nirmala).

The pure Consciousness liberated, eternal, without desires and thoughts, unchanging and without form. It is without attributes.

35. Like the space I fill all things within and without. Changeless and the same in all, at all times I am pure, unattached, stainless and motionless.

36. I am verily that Supreme Brahman alone which is Eternal, Pure and Free, One, indivisible and non-dual and of the nature of Changeless-Knowledge- Infinite.

37. The impression "I am Brahman" thus created by constant practice destroys ignorance and the agitation caused by it, just as medicine or Rasayana destroys disease.

Rasayana is an Ayurvedic technique to prolong life and strengthen the body.

38. Sitting in a solitary place, freeing the mind from desires and controlling the senses, meditate with unswerving attention on the Atman which is One without-a-second.

Brahman - Atman is often called "One without-a-second" (Ekam advitîyam) which means that, "only Brahman is", or that, "everything is Brahman". There is nothing else before or after Brahman, which is eternal.

The described meditation method can lead to the state of consciousness Samadhi.

39. The wise one should intelligently merge the entire world-of-objects in the Atman alone and constantly think of Atman ever as contaminated by anything as the sky.

To relate the whole world ie. the relative existence to Atman gives the opportunity to distinguish the real from the illusion.

40. He who has realised the Supreme, discards all his identification with the objects of names and forms. (Thereafter) he dwells as an embodiment of the Infinite Consciousness and Bliss. He becomes the Self.

He who has realized the highest is aware in Consciousness – Atman. This is Bliss that surpasses all sense pleasures.

41. There are no distinctions such as "Knower", the "Knowledge" and the "Object of Knowledge" in the Supreme Self. On account of Its being of the nature of endless Bliss, It does not admit of such distinctions within Itself. It alone shines by Itself.

Atman - The Self is beyond all distinctions. It is the Jivan which is involved in various distinctions, with the ultimate aim of becoming aware of Atman.

42. When this the lower and the higher aspects of the Self are well churned together, the fire of knowledge is born from it, which in its mighty conflagration shall burn down all the fuel of ignorance in us.

When one is mature, ignorance is destroyed with the fire of knowledge. The lower aspects of ignorance are annihilated and replaced by higher aspects of Knowledge and awareness.

43. The Lord of the early dawn (Aruna) himself has already looted away the thick darkness, when soon the sun rises. The Divine Consciousness of the Self rises when the right knowledge has already killed the darkness in the bosom.

Aruna was the son of sage Kashyapa. He is described in the work The Mahabharata.

44. Atman is an ever-present reality. Yet, because of ignorance it is not realised. On the destruction of ignorance Atman is realised. It is like the missing ornament of one's neck.

Atman is always present, through conscious presence it is confirmed.

45. Brahman appears to be a 'Jiva' because of ignorance, just as a post appears to be a ghost. The ego-centric-individuality is destroyed when the real nature of the 'Jiva' is realised as the Self.

The ego fades away as Atman is realized and becomes conscious. However, the ego and the mind will always be there for the necessities of practical life.

46. The ignorance characterised by the notions 'I' and 'Mine' is destroyed by the knowledge produced by the realisation of the true nature of the Self, just as right information removes the wrong notion about the directions.

The one who is no longer identified with "I" and "mine", does not get caught in the trap of dualism, but goes in his own direction.

47. The Yogi of perfect realisation and enlightenment sees through his "eye of wisdom" (Gyana Chakshush) the entire universe in his own Self and regards everything else as his own Self and nothing else.

The Yogi who is rooted in Consciousness has access to the Divine Wisdom through Atman .

48. Nothing whatever exists other than the Atman: the tangible universe is verily Atman. As pots and jars are verily made of clay and cannot be said to be anything but clay, so too, to the enlightened soul and that is perceived is the Self.

Being present in Consciousness means that everything is perceived as Atman.

49. A liberated one, endowed with Self-knowledge, gives up the traits of his previously explained equipments (Upadhis) and because of his nature of Satchitananda, he verily becomes Brahman like (the worm that grows to be a wasp).

Presence in Consciousness changes existence from being bound to the relative to being established in Sat-Chit-Ananda (Truth-Consciousness-Bliss). Relative existence is then no longer attractive and has lost its appeal.

50. After crossing the ocean of delusion and killing the monsters of likes and dislikes, the Yogi who is united with peace dwells in the glory of his own realised Self – as an Atmaram.

The sutra refers to the opus Ramayana, where Rama is described as established in the Self. "After crossing the sea of delusion and slaying monsters" is said to refer to the sea dividing Ceylon and India and a bridge was erected for Rama to defeat the demon Ravana. This can be seen as Rama having to cross the ocean of illusion to defeat the evil and dark energies.

51. The self-abiding Jivan Mukta, relinquishing all his attachments to the illusory external happiness and satisfied with the bliss derived from the Atman, shines inwardly like a lamp placed inside a jar.

When the level of awareness derived from Atman asserts itself, the Jivan Mukta (the liberated one) is so completely satisfied that the illusory external happiness has no attraction.

52. Though he lives in the conditionings (Upadhis), he, the contemplative one, remains ever unconcerned with anything or he may move about like the wind, perfectly unattached.

Being anchored and present in Consciousness means that despite the influence of conceptual existence, one can still be unaffected and unbound.

53. On the destruction of the Upadhis, the contemplative one is totally absorbed in 'Vishnu', the All-pervading Spirit, like water into water, space into space and light into light.

It becomes equally obvious that the one who is freed from the Upadhis becomes established on a level of awareness that includes the "All Pervading Spirit," as water to water, space to space, and light to light.

54. Realise That to be Brahman, the attainment of which leaves nothing more to be attained, the blessedness of which leaves no other blessing to be desired and the knowledge of which leaves nothing more to be known.

When Brahmanconsciousness is established, the highest is attained. then there is nothing more to achieve.

55. Realise that to be Brahman which, when seen, leaves nothing more to be seen, which having become one is not born again in this world and which, when knowing leaves nothing else to be known.

When Brahman (Consciousness) is established, the highest is attained, then there is no more knowledge to be gained. There is then no reason to be born again.

56. Realise that to be Brahman which is Existence-Knowledge-Bliss-Absolute, which is Non-dual, Infinite, Eternal and One and which fills all the quarters – above and below and all that exists between.

*Sarvam khalvidam brahma – 'all this is Brahman' (Chando-
gya Upanishad 3.14.1). Brahman includes all worlds and all
existence in eternity.*

57. Realise that to be Brahman which is Non-dual, Indivisible, One and Blissful and which is indicated in Vedanta
as the Immutable Substratum, realised after the negation of
all tangible objects.

*"Neti neti" is the method (negation) of distinguishing the
parts from the whole and arriving at the conclusion that
only the unchanging Substratum which is Brahman has real
existence.*

58. Deities like Brahma and others taste only a particle, of
the unlimited Bliss of Brahman and enjoy in proportion
their share of that particle.

*Gods like Brahma manifest and administer parts of existen-
ce's unlimited energy supply.*

59. All objects are pervaded by Brahman. All actions are
possible because of Brahman: therefore Brahman permeates everything as butter permeates milk.

Brahmanconsciousness pervades everything while the mind and sense organs are limited.

60. Realise that to be Brahman which is neither subtle nor gross: neither short nor long: without birth or change: without form, qualities, colour and name.

Since Brahman has no qualities, it means that the mind and sense organs do not have the opportunity to experience Brahman based on the mind's ability

61. That by the light of which the luminous, orbs like the Sun and the Moon are illuminated, but which is not illumined by their light, realise that to be Brahman.

The light of the moon comes from the sun and the sun produces its own light, but the basis of all light comes from Brahman (Consciousness).

62. Pervading the entire universe outwardly and in wardly the Supreme Brahman shines of Itself like the fire that permeates a red-hot iron-ball and glows by itself.

63. Brahman is other than this, the universe. There exists nothing that is not Brahman. If any object other than Brahman appears to exist, it is unreal like the mirage.

Brahman exists as non-dualistic Being. Anything other than Brahman cannot have a real existence but can be regarded as an unreal dualistic mirage and can be seen as dream awareness. The paradox is that even the unreal dualistic mirage and a dream is based on ignorance, is Brahman, otherwise Brahman could not be everything.

64. All that is perceived, or heard, is Brahman and nothing else. Attaining the knowledge of the Reality, one sees the Universe as the non-dual Brahman, Existence-Knowledge-Bliss-Absolute.

"Sarvam Khalvidam Brahma"– 'all is Brahman, or "Ekam Eva Advitiyam Brahma" Brahman is One and is the only one without a second's hesitation.

65. Though Atman is Pure Consciousness and ever present everywhere, yet It is perceived by the eye-of-wisdom alone: but one whose vision is obscured by ignorance he does not see It; as the blind do not see the resplendent Sun.

To be established in the "eye of wisdom" means to have experienced beyond the limitations of the mind and at the same time gained an understanding that existence has dimensions beyond the mind. This awakening enables the presence of Atman the pure Consciousness.

66. The 'Jiva' free from impurities, being heated in the fire of knowledge kindled by hearing and so on, shines of itself like gold.

To become free from bodily and mental impurities one can perform Tapas ie. various exercises such as; Yoga- Asanas (body exercises), Pranayama (spiritual exercises) and various Mudras (purification exercises).

67. The Atman, the Sun of Knowledge that rises in the sky of the heart, destroys the darkness of the ignorance, pervades and sustains all and shines and makes everything to shine.

Being permanently present in Consciousness means true knowledge is established and the darkness of ignorance is dispelled and enlightenment is established.

68. He who renouncing all activities, who is free of all the limitations of time, space and direction, worships his own Atman which is present everywhere, which is the destroyer of heat and cold, which is Bliss-Eternal and stainless, becomes All-knowing and All-pervading and attains thereafter Immortality.

To renouncing all activities, is not to be bound by the activities that must be done.

Thus concludes Atma-Bodha. Om shanti shanti shanti!

Aparokshanubhuti
Self-realization

by

Sri Adi Shankara
Shankaracharya

Translation & comments
Jan Fahleman

Preface

Aparokshanubhuti was written by Adi Shankara, probably in the early 8th century, with the aim of explaining the non-dualistic philosophy of Advaita Vedanta. It describes a method that seekers can follow to experience the truth through the removal of the ignorance that hides the truth.

Paroksha means 'that which is far away'; 'a' means 'that which is near': it refers to the 'nearest of the nearest', the Self, Atman which is non-dualistic. It can also be translated as "direct realization" or "immediate realization", meaning realization without the need for any "media" or object. Anubhuti means to realize, to experience. So the word means "self-realization". Such realization differs from the knowledge of objects through sense perception, inference or blind faith.

The text consists of 144 verses. It is part of the Prakarana Grantha, which is a collection of scriptures or Upanishads written by teachers or spiritual masters, which should help to increase the understanding of Vedanta.

1. I bow down to Him - to Sri Hari (the destroyer of ignorance), the Supreme Bliss, the First Teacher, Ishwara, the All-pervading One and the Cause of all Lokas (the universe).

The devotion is directed towards God, Ishwara who is present everywhere and is the cause of all causes.

2. Herein is expounded (the means of attaining to) Aparokshanubhuti (Self-Realization) for the acquisition of final liberation. Only the pure in heart should constantly and with all effort meditate upon the truth herein taught.

To achieve Self-Realization, meditation is an aid that gives a pure heart and final liberation.

3. The four preliminary qualifications (the means to the attainment of knowledge), such as Vairagya (dispassion) and the like, are acquired by men by propitiating Hari (the

Lord), through austerities and the performance of duties pertaining to their social order and stage in life.

These four qualifications are; detachment from the relative illusory existence, discernment of the real and the unreal, mind control and longing for liberation (enlightenment).

4. The indifference with which one treats the excreta of a crow - such an indifference to all objects of enjoyment from the realm of Brahma to this world (in view of their perishable nature), is verily called pure Vairagya.

Non-attachment to desire for sense sensations must be established at a level of awareness that is naturally established in the awareness of the individual. From this level of awareness the individual observes the sense sensations and the relative objects.

5. Atman (the seer) in itself is alone permanent, the seen is opposed to it (ie. transient) – such a settled conviction is truly known as discrimination.

Atman which is; absolute eternal, unchanging, pure Consciousness, is opposed to the relative perceptible mind and

*intellect. By being consciously present in Atman, the absolute
and the relative can be distinguished and witnessed.*

5

6. Abandonment of desires at all times is called Shama and
restraint of the external functions of the organs is called
Dama.

*Not letting the sense sensations take over presence in awa-
reness means the desire for the sense sensations must be
controllable.*

7. Turning away completely from all sense-objects is the
height of Uparati, and patient endurance of all sorrow or
pain is known as Titiksha which is conducive to happiness.

*Not allowing the sense objects to take over the presence of
awareness is called Uparati and being patient and enduring
in the face of sorrow and pain is called Titiksha.*

8. Implicit faith in the words of the Vedas and the teachers
(who interpret them) is known as Shraddha, and concentration of the mind on the only object Sat (i.e. Brahman) is
regarded as Samadhana.

Having faith in and being fully present in the Vedas and in the Sat ie. the truth is to be established in the one ie. Brahman, this can be considered as Samadhana.

9. When and how shall I, O Lord, be free from the bonds of this world (i.e. births and deaths) – such a burning desire is called Mumukshuta.

In relative existence there are constant changes such as birth and death. To be freed from the mundane and the cycle of birth and death requires a burning desire to be freed to finally be present and established in Consciousness.

10. Only that person who is in possession of the said qualification (as means to Knowledge) should constantly reflect with a view to attaining Knowledge, desiring his own good.

To constantly reflect on what is truth and what is illusion, in order to be freed through knowledge from what is untrue and unreal.

11. Knowledge is not brought about by any other means than Vichara, just as an object is nowhere perceived (seen) without the help of light.

Asking and reflecting (Vichara) is the basis for acquiring knowledge.

12. Who am I? How is this (world) created? Who is its creator? Of what material is this (world) made? This is the way of that Vichara (enquiry).

Asking these existential questions activates knowledge about existence.

13. I am neither the body, a combination of the (five elements (of matter), nor am I an aggregate of the senses; I am something different from these. This is the way of that Vichara.

That by asking the question; Who am I?, experience and knowledge can arise from the fact that Atman is neither, body, mind or the relative existence.

14. Everything is produced by ignorance, and dissolves in the wake of Knowledge. The various thoughts (modifications of Antahkarana) must be the creator. Such is this Vichara.

Through the awakened conscious mind (Antahkarana) arises Knowledge.

15. The material (cause) of these two (i.e., ignorance and thought) is the One (without a second), subtle (not apprehended by the senses) and unchanging Sat (Existence), just as the earth is the material (cause) of the pot and the like. This is the way of that Vichara.

The true existence Sat is the cause of causes and unattached to the senses.

16. As I am also the One, the Subtle, the Knower, the Witness, the Ever-Existent, and the Unchanging, so there is no doubt that I am "That" (i.e. Brahman). Such is this enquiry.

The Self that is "That" is Brahman, the absolute pure Consciousness, the One, the Subtle, the Knowledge, the Witness, the Ever-Existing Existence and the Immutable.

17. Atman is verily one and without parts, whereas the body consists of many parts; and yet the people see (confound) these two as one ! What else can be called ignorance but this?

Atman the absolute Consciousness, is characterized by being in unity with total existence and independent of time, space and relative existence. As long as one is bound to the relative mind, one believes that one is the body, the mind, and the relative illusion of existence and thus ignorant of the truth. Godconsciousness is everything and in unity with everything ie. both the reality and the relative illusion.

18. Atman is the ruler of the body and is internal, the body is the ruled and is external; and yet, etc.

The one who experiences the mind must have experienced the Atman to understand what rules and governs the body.

19. Atman is all Consciousness and holy, the body is all flesh and impure; and yet, etc.

There is only one Consciousness (Atman), it is sacred and eternal unlike the body which can be considered relative and ever changing.

20. Atman is the (supreme) Illuminator and purity itself; the body is said to be of the nature of darkness; and yet, etc.

*Atman ie. the pure Consciousness is the eternal absolute
which is not perishable as the material body is.*

21. Atman is eternal, since it is Existence itself; the body is
transient, as it is non-existence in essence; and yet etc.

*Atman is eternal and unchanging while the body is subject
to change; as birth, maintenance and death.*

22. The luminosity of Atman consists in the manifestation
of all objects. Its luminosity is not like that of fire or any
such thing, for (in spite of the presence of such lights)
darkness prevails at night (at some place or other).

*The effulgence of the Atman cannot be compared with any
worldly light. It is an inner light that can only be experienced
mentally, regardless of whether there is darkness or light in
the surroundings.*

23. How strange is it that a person ignorantly rests con-
tented with the idea that he is the body, while he knows it
as something belonging to him (and therefore apart from
him) even as a person who sees a pot (knows it as apart
from him)!

24. I am verily Brahman, being equanimous, quiescent,
and by nature absolute Existence, Knowledge, and Bliss. I
am not the body which is nonexistence itself. This is called
true Knowledge by the wise.

*Everything is Brahman. He who is present in Brahman is ba-
lanced, wise and able to distinguish the real from the unreal.
Being present in Brahman is not based on belief, or experience only on Being.*

25. I am without any change, without any form, free from
all blemish and decay. I am not the body which is non-existence itself.

*To be present in God Consciousness is to be present in a state
of awareness where there is no change, no material forms
that can decay.*

26. I am not subjected to any disease, I am beyond all comprehension, free from all alternatives and all-pervading. I am not the body which is nonexistence itself. If the body becomes ill, it is not the Self but the body that is sick, as the Self is separated from the body. The Self is not dependent on intellectual alternatives and beyond all thought and all relativity.

27. I am without any attribute or activity, I am eternal, ever free, and imperishable. I am not the body which is non-existence itself.

Atman exists without any relative concepts or qualities, imperishable and free in a constant now.

28. I am free from all impurity, I am immovable, unlimited, holy, un-decaying, and immortal. I am not the body which is non-existence itself.

The absolute pure Consciousness, Atman is unlimited in time and space and immortal.

29. O you ignorant one ! Why do you assert the blissful, ever-existent Atman, which resides in your own body and

is (evidently) different from it, which is known as Purusha
and is established (by the Shruti as identical with Brahman), to be absolutely non-existent?

*If one is aware in the relative mind and ego, then Atman is
without qualities. It is only when one is present in Atman
(which is identical with Brahman, God Consciousness) that
one can relate to Atman as reality or Being.*

30. O you ignorant one ! Try to know, with the help of
Shruti and reasoning, your own Self, Purusha, which is
different from the body, (not a void but) the very form of
existence, and very difficult for persons like you to realize.

*If one lacks awareness in Godconsciousness, it can be dif-
ficult to understand the true eternal Self, even if it is your
Being.*

31. The Supreme (Purusha) known as "I" (ego) is but one,
whereas the gross bodies are many. So how can this body
be Purusha?

*Purusha or Godconsciousness encompasses everything,
including the body.*

32. "I" (ego) is well established as the subject of perception whereas the body is the object. This is learnt from the fact that when we speak of the body we say, "This is mine." So how can this body be Purusha?

There is a big difference between realizing that I am the body versus realizing that the body is an aid that I use.

33. It is a fact of direct experience that the "I" (Atman) is without any change, whereas the body is always undergoing changes. So how can this body be Purusha?

Purusha, Godconsciousness encompasses all, ie. even everything manifested and then also the body.

34. Wise men have ascertained the (real) nature of Purusha from that Shruti text, "(There is nothing) higher than He (Purusha)," etc. So how can this body be Purusha?

The shruti text referred to is in the Svetasvataraupanishad.

35. Again the Shruti has declared in the Purusha Sukta that "All this is verily the Purusha". So how can this body be Purusha?

Purusha is the Godconsciousness which is both the eternal Being and the perishable temporary illusion.

36. So also it is said in Brihadaranyaka that "The Purusha is completely unattached". How can this body wherein inhere innumerable impurities be the Purusha?

Purusha is unmoved before the manifested existence and at the same time present in it.

37. There again it is clearly stated that "the Purusha is self-illumined". So how can the body which is inert (insentient) and illumined by an external agent be the Purusha?

Purusha is everything, both the conceptual and beyond the concepts, both that which is enlightened by itself and that which is enlightened by an external factor.

38. Moreover, the Karma-kanda also declares that the Atman is different from the body and permanent, as it endures even after the fall of the body and reaps the fruits of actions (done in this life).

39. Even the subtle body consists of many parts and is unstable. It is also an object of perception, is changeable, limited and non-existent by nature. So how can this be the Purusha?

Beginning in sutra 31, Shankara asks the question; how can the relative body be at the same time the absolute Purusha? The answer to the question is entirely dependent on which state of awareness prevails. The purpose of the question is to start a process that will hopefully lead to an awakening and a presence in Purusha.

40. The immutable Atman, the substratum of the ego, is thus different from these two bodies, and is the Purusha, the Ishwara (the Lord of all), the Self of all; It is present in every form and yet transcends them all.

The physical and the astral body are in constant change and thus belong to relative existence. Purusha who encompasses the totality also encompasses these bodies.

41. Thus the enunciation of the difference between the Atman and the body has (indirectly) asserted, indeed, after the manner of the Tarkashastra, the reality of the pheno

menal world. But what end of human life is served thereby?

Whether the relative existence is true and real depends entirely on the state of awareness of the observer. Therefore, it is meaningless to talk about true or false in this case.

42. Thus the view that the body is the Atman has been denounced by the enunciation of the difference between the Atman and the body. Now is clearly stated the unreality of the difference between the two.

It is clear that the Atman and the body belong together and are one and the same.

43. No division in Consciousness is admissible at any time as it is always one and the same. Even the individuality of the Jiva must be known as false, like the delusion of a snake in a rope.

The individuality of the Jiva in the form of mind, ego and intellect must also be seen as Consciousness.

44. As through the ignorance of the real nature of the rope the very rope appears in an instant as a snake, so also does pure Consciousness appear in the form of the phenomenal universe without undergoing any change. Consciousness is unaffected by the changing phenomenal relative illusion that exists due to ignorance.

45. There exists no other material cause of this phenomenal universe except Brahman. Hence this whole universe is but Brahman and nothing else.

Everything is Brahman, both the relative and the absolute are Brahman, there is no duality or any exception.

46. From such declaration (of the Shruti) as "All this is Atman", it follows that the idea of the pervaded and the pervading is illusory. This supreme truth being realized, where is the room for any distinction between the cause and the effect?

When the truth is revealed, the dualistic illusion is understood and need not be questioned.

47. Certainly the Shruti has directly denied manifoldness in Brahman. The non-dual cause being an established fact, how could the phenomenal universe be different from It?

Since dualistic existence is an illusion, the relative universe must also be a dualistic illusion. Only Brahman ie. Consciousness is.

48. Moreover, the Shruti has condemned (the belief in variety) in the words, "The person who", being deceived by Maya, "sees variety in this (Brahman), goes from death to death".

He who is bound by the belief that Brahman is only relative and manifold, is bewildered by Maya (the intellectual mind dependent on the relative illusion) and is then forced to incarnate until he realizes the truth; that Brahman is non-dualistic.

49. Inasmuch as all beings are born of Brahman, the supreme Atman, they must be understood to be verily Brahman.

As everything is Brahman, the creation, maintenance and dissolution of creation is Brahman.

50. The Shruti has clearly declared that Brahman alone is the substratum of all varieties of names, forms and actions.

51. Just as a thing made of gold ever has the nature of gold, so also a being born of Brahman has always the nature of Brahman.

Brahman always exists as eternal and unchanging in the relative existence.

52. Fear is attributed to the ignorant one who rests after making even the slightest distinction between the Jivatman and the Paramatman.

He who is present in the Paramatman has nothing to fear as he is not in conflict with anything but is one with everything.

53. When duality appears through ignorance, one sees another; but when everything becomes identified with the Atman, one does not perceive another even in the least.

How existence is perceived depends entirely on the state of awareness one is in. Living in the duality of the mind (Jivat-man) means that the relative existence colors the experience and when the non-dualistic Atman is present in the awareness, it is the pure absolute Consciousness that illuminates the experience.

54. In that state when one realizes all as identified with the Atman, there arises neither delusion nor sorrow, in consequence of the absence of duality.

Since there is no duality there is no conflict or enmity, nothing that can be an obstacle as everything is in unity.

55. The Shruti in the form of the Brihadaranyaka has declared that this Atman, which is the Self of all, is verily Brahman.

Since there is no duality there is no conflict or enmity, nothing that can be an obstacle as everything is in unity.

56. This world, though an object of our daily experience and serving all practical purposes, is, like the dream world, of the nature of non-existence, inasmuch as it is contradicted the next moment.

Existence is real only in the present. The past and the future are unreal just like a dream.

57. The dream (experience) is unreal in waking, whereas the waking (experience) is absent in dream. Both, however, are non-existent in deep sleep which, again, is not experienced in either.

Experiences are always dualistic as there is someone experiencing and something being experienced. In deep sleep there is neither anyone who experiences nor anything to experience.

58. Thus all the three states are unreal inasmuch as they are the creation of the three Gunas; but their witness (the reality behind them) is, beyond all Gunas, eternal, one, and is Consciousness itself.

The three gunas are three different states of relative existence. Tamas is inertia, cruelty and low energy, rajas is activity, desire and active energy, satva is goodness, truth and pure energy. These relative states exist temporarily while Consciousness is constantly and eternally present.

59. Just as (after the illusion has gone) one is no more deluded to see a jar in earth or silver in the nacre, so does one no more see Jiva in Brahman when the latter is realized (as one's own Self).

When duality does not influence and mislead, one sees reality and truth. One sees that the pot is actually clay and the Jivan is actually Brahman.

60. Just as earth is described as a jar, gold as an ear-ring, and a nacre as silver, so is Brahman described as Jiva.

Praktiti, the relative conceptual nature, can be observed and an awakening can take place whereby illusion and reality merge into the truth that all is Brahman.

61. Just as blueness in the sky, water in the mirage, and a human figure in a post (are but illusory), so is the universe in Atman.

The illusory relative and the absolute Atman exist in non-dualism.

62. Just as the appearance of a ghost in an empty place, of a castle in the air, and of a second moon in the sky (is illusory), so is the appearance of the universe in Brahman.

63. Just as it is water that appears as ripples and waves, or again it is copper, that appears in the form of vessel so it is Atman that appears as the whole universe.

Beyond the relative form there is always the absolute Atman.

64. Just as it is earth that appears under the name of a jar, or it is threads that appear under the name of a cloth, so it is Atman that appears under the name of the universe. This Atman is to be known by negating the names.

The universe is the conceptual relative which has name and form and is not to be confused with Atman which is without these attributes.

65. People perform all their actions in and through Brahman, (but on account of ignorance they are not aware of that), just as through ignorance persons do not know that jars and other earthenwares are nothing but earth.

Reality and truth are dependent on the prevailing state of awareness. Only Brahman is real and true.

66. Just as there ever exist the relation of cause and effect between earth and a jar, so does the same relation exist between Brahman and the phenomenal world; this has been established here on the strength of scriptural texts and reasoning.

67. Just as (Consciousness of) earth forces itself upon our mind while thinking of a jar, so also does (the idea of) ever-shining Brahman flash on us while contemplating on the phenomenal world.

There is always a relationship between what is consciously present and the prevailing state of awareness. Being able to look at the phenomenal world and Brahman at the same time requires an awareness that can experience the relative and the absolute existence at the same time.

68. Atman, though ever pure (to a wise man), always appears to be impure (to an ignorant one), just as a rope always appears in two different ways to a knowing person and an ignorant one.

In the dark a rope is perceived as a snake, but in the light it is obvious that it is a rope. What has changed is not the rope but the experience of the rope. In the same way, it is then that Atman (which is not the mind), is misunderstood due to ignorance, to be the mind.

69. Just as a jar is all earth, so also is the body all Consciousness. The division, therefore, into the Self and non-Self is made by the ignorant to no purpose.

As everything is Consciousness, the division of Self and non-Self is only ignorance. From sutras 70 to 86, Sankara describes various illusions and misinterpretations to compare with how a person due to ignorance mistakes the relationship between the Atman and the body. Being caught in the relative view of the mind often results in ignorance of the totality of existence.

70. Just as a rope is imagined to be a snake and a nacre to be a piece of silver, so is the Atman determined to be the body by an ignorant person.

71. Just as earth is thought of as a jar (made of it) and threads as a cloth, so is Atman, so is the Atman determined to be the body by an ignorant person.

72. Just as gold is thought of as an ear-ring and water as waves, so is the Atman determined to be the body by an ignorant person.

73. Just as the stump of a tree is mistaken for a human figure and a mirage for water, so is the Atman, so is the Atman determined to be the body by an ignorant person.

74. Just as a mass of wood work is thought of as a house and iron as a sword, so is the Atman determined to be the body by an ignorant person.

75. Just as one sees the illusion of a tree on account of water, so does a person on account of ignorance see Atman as the body.

76. Just as to a person going in a boat everything appears to be in motion, so is the Atman determined to be the body by an ignorant person.

77. Just as to a person suffering from a defect (jaundice) white things appear as yellow, so is the Atman determined to be the body by an ignorant person.

78. Just as to a person with defective eyes everything appears to be defective, so is the Atman determined to be the body by an ignorant person.

79. Just as a firebrand, through mere rotation, appears circular like the sun, so is the Atman determined to be the body by an ignorant person.

80. Just as all things that are really large appear to be very small owing to great distance, so is the Atman determined to be the body by an ignorant person.

81. Just as all objects that are very small appear to be large when viewed through lenses, so does one, so is the Atman determined to be the body by an ignorant person.

82. Just as a surface of glass is mistaken for water, or vice versa, so is the Atman determined to be the body by an ignorant person.

83. Just as a person imagines a jewel in fire or vice versa, so is the Atman determined to be the body by an ignorant person.

84. Just as when clouds move, the moon appears to be in motion, so is the Atman determined to be the body by an ignorant person.

85. Just as a person through confusion loses all distinction between the different points of the compass, so is the Atman determined to be the body by an ignorant person.

86. Just as the moon (when reflected) in water appears to one as unsteady, so does one, so is the Atman determined to be the body by an ignorant person.

87. Thus through ignorance arises in Atman the delusion of the body, which, again, through Self-realization, disappears in the supreme Atman.

Presence in Atman dispels all ignorance and the relationship between Atman and the body.

88. When the whole universe, movable and immovable, is known to be Atman, and thus the existence of everything else is negated, where is then any room to say that the body is Atman?

When one realizes that the total non-dual existence is Atman, the body must also be included. The body as separated from the Atman does not exist but as a mental dualistic illusion.

89. O enlightened one, pass your time always contemplating on Atman while you are experiencing all the results of Prarabdha; for it ill becomes you to feel distressed.

To be constantly present in Atman means that one realizes that what karma has resulted in does not affect the absolute Consciousness ie. Atman.

90. The theory one hears of from the scripture, that Prarabdha does not lose its hold upon one even after the origination of the knowledge of Atman, is now being refuted.

Conscious presence in Atman means liberation from all Karma (Prarabdha) of the past.

91. After the origination of the knowledge of Reality, Prarabdha verily ceases to exist, inasmuch as the body and the like become non-existent; just as a dream does not exist on waking.

The dream state of awareness and the waking state of awareness are two different states of awareness that are experienced as real. When Atman is experienced, it is felt that this state of awareness is the only real state of awareness ie. the awareness of Consciousness. Presence in Consciousness generates no dualistic experiences and thus no karma.

92. That Karma which is done in a previous life is known as Prarabdha (which produces the present life). But such Karma cannot take the place of Prarabdha (for a man of knowledge), as he has no other birth (being free from ego).

For one who has knowledge of Atman, karma has no function to fulfill.

93. Just as the body in a dream is superimposed (and therefore illusory), so is also this body. How could there be any birth of the superimposed (body), and in the absence of birth (of the body) where is the room for that (i.e, Prarabdha) at all?

From the relative existence of the body there is Prarabha, but from absolute Atman there is no birth in any body and thus no karma (i.e. Prarabdha). Since the ego does not generate wishes and desires, there is no need for any manifestation and therefore no need for rebirth.

94. The Vedanta texts declare ignorance to be verily the material (cause) of the phenomenal world just as earth is of a jar. That (ignorance) being destroyed, where can the universe subsist?

Relative existence has an existence as long as ignorance exists. Vedanta can provide an explanation of the difference between absolute and relative existence. Vedanta destroys ignorance.

95. Just as a person out of confusion perceives only the snake leaving aside the rope, so does an ignorant person see only the phenomenal world without knowing the reality.

Depending only on the mind and intellect gives a limited perception of existence and reality.

96. The real nature of the rope being known, the appearance of the snake no longer persists; so the substratum being known, the phenomenal world disappears completely.

When reality shows itself, the illusion can no longer be credible.

97. The body also being within the phenomenal world (and therefore unreal), how could Prarabdha exist? It is, therefore, for the understanding of the ignorant alone that the Shruti speaks of Prarabdha.

As long as one identifies with body, mind and the phenomenal world, Prarabdha also automatically exists. In the relative existence there is constant change, and what happen gives Prarabdha cause and effect in time and space.

98. "And all the actions of a man perish when he realizes that (Atman) which is both the higher and the lower". Here the clear use of the plural by the Shruti is to negate Prarabdha as well.

Presence in Atman implies non-dualism, then everything is united as one and Prarabdha do not apply.

99. If the ignorant still arbitrarily maintain this, they will not only involve themselves into two absurdities but will also run the risk of forgoing the Vedantic conclusion. So one should accept those Shrutis alone from which proceeds true knowledge.

100. Now, for the attainment of the aforesaid (knowledge), I shall expound the fifteen steps by the help of which one should practice profound meditation at all times.

101. The Atman that is absolute existence and knowledge cannot be realized without constant practice. So one seeking after knowledge should long meditate upon Brahman for the attainment of the desired goal.

Spiritual exercises such as meditation provide insights and knowledge about existence ie. Brahman.

102-103. The steps, in order, are described as follows: the control of the senses, the control of the mind, renunciation, silence, space, time, posture, the restraining root (Mulabandha), the equipoise of the body, the firmness of vision, the control of the vital forces, the withdrawal of the mind, concentration, self-contemplation and complete absorption.

Shankara's Fifteen Steps to Knowledge and Self-Realization;

1. Control of the senses. Implies control of the sensual desires.
2. Control of the mind. To use the mind as a tool, without identify with the ego and the intellect. To divert the mind from sense object (pratyahara).
3. Renunciation – being able to give up something that attracts the mind.
4. Silence – being able to be present in silence ie. without active sound.
5. Space – accepting the unlimited Being.
6. Time – realizing that time is one of man-made relative measures.
7. Posture – maintaining a vital and powerful posture through Yoga asanas.
8. The restraining root (Mulabandha) – being anchored in the chakra muladhara, which provides a fundamental stability.
9. The body's equilibrium – to give the body a balanced energy supplement.
10. Firmness of vision – that the five senses should be strong and functional.
11. Control of the vital forces – taking control of prana with the help of pranayama.
12. The withdrawal of the mind – not being bound by the mind.
13. Concentration – being consciously present (dharana).

14. Self-contemplation – meditating (dhyana)

15. Complete absorption – being consciously present in Atman (Samadhi).

104. The restraint of all the senses by means of such knowledge as "All this is Brahman" is rightly called Yama, which should be practiced again and again.

Yama is knowledge and rules of living that lead to purity and harmony and is rooted in universal wisdom.

105. The continuous flow of only one kind of thought to the exclusion of all other thoughts, is called Niyama, which is verily the supreme bliss and is regularly practiced by the wise.

Niyama are rules of living to achieve; purity, contentment, self-discipline, self-study and surrender to God, thereby facilitating conscious presence in Consciousness.

106. The abandonment of the illusory universe by realizing it as the allconscious Atman is the real renunciation honored by the great, since it is of the nature of immediate liberation.

Transcending (abandoning the illusory universe) means immediate liberation as reality is revealed.

107. The wise should always be one with that silence wherefrom words together with the mind turn back without reaching it, but which is attainable by the Yogins.

The mind and thoughts are limited to relative existence and cannot be present in the silence experienced by a Yogi in Samadhi.

108-109. Who can describe That (i.e., Brahman) whence words turn away? (So silence is inevitable while describing Brahman). Or if the phenomenal world were to be described, even that is beyond words. This, to give an alternate definition, may also be termed silence known among the sages as congenital. The observance of silence by restraining speech, on the other hand, is ordained by the teachers of Brahman for the ignorant.

Both the absolute Consciousness (Brahman) and the relative phenomenal world (maya) can never be described by either thoughts or words. Only the wise who have dispelled ignorance can be present in the silence (inactivity) that is beyond thought and words. Stillness and silence ie. inactivity is the basis of activity. Being consciously united with Consciousness automatically brings stillness and silence.

110. That solitude is known as space, wherein the universe does not exist in the beginning, end or middle, but whereby it is pervaded at all times.

The eternal limitless space is constantly permeated with Consciousness.

111. The non-dual (Brahman) that is bliss indivisible is denoted by the word 'time', since it brings into existence, in the twinkling of an eye all beings from Brahman downwards.

The creation of all beings takes place beyond the influence of time by Brahman.

112. One should known that as real posture in which the meditation on Brahman flows spontaneously and unceasingly, and not any other that destroys one's happiness.

It is important to sit in a comfortable pose during meditation, in order to be spontaneously present in Consciousness and not let anything else take over the attention. The lotus position (padmasana) is considered by many to be the best position for long meditation sessions, but the important thing is that the pose does not cause discomfort and pain that takes attention.

113. That which is well known as the origin of all beings and the support of the whole universe, which is immutable and in which the enlightened are completely merged ... that alone is known as Siddhasana (eternal Brahman).

114. That (Brahman) which is the root of all existence and on which the restraint of the mind is based is called the restraining root (Mulabandha) which should always be adopted since it is fit for Raja-yogins.

It can be important to have some support when the mind must be held back in abstinence. For a yogi who seeks presence in Consciousness (Brahman), it is a security to lean on that which is the root of all existence.

115. Absorption in the uniform Brahman should be known as the equipoise of the limbs (Dehasamya). Other

wise mere straightening of the body like that of a dried-up tree is no equipoise.

Being present in Brahman brings balance and vitality both spiritually and physically.

116. Converting the ordinary vision into one of knowledge one should view the world as Brahman itself. That is the noblest vision, and not that which is directed to the tip of the nose.

It is often said that "you can't see further than your nose" i.e. that one has a limited point of view. That is when one is bound to the mind and not present in Brahman ie. in Cons-ciousness.

117. Or, one should direct one's vision to That alone where all distinction of the seer, sight, and the seen ceases and not to the tip of the nose.

When the limited experience of the mind ceases, "It" ie. beco-mes Consciousness present.

118. The restraint of all modifications of the mind by regarding all mental states like the Chitta as Brahman alone, is called Pranayama.

Performing the breathing exercise Pranayama means that the (pranan) breath helps the conscious attention to release all mental states (Citta) and be aware off Brahman.

119-120. The negation of the phenomenal world is known as Rechaka (breathing out), the thought, "I am verily Brahman", is called Puraka (breathing in), and the steadiness of that thought thereafter is called Kumbhaka (restraining the breath). This is the real course of Pranayama for the enlightened, whereas the ignorant only torture the nose. The purpose of Pranayama is to activate the Prana (life force) to become present in Consciousness.

121. The absorption of the mind in the Supreme Consciousness by realizing Atman in all objects is known as Pratyahara (withdrawal of the mind) which should be practiced by the seekers after liberation.

Being present in Atman means that the mind no longer dominates awareness (Pratyahara). This automatically results in presence in the Divine Consciousness.

122. The steadiness of the mind through realization of Brahman wherever the mind goes, is known as the supreme Dharana (concentration).

Pratyahara takes the conscious presence from the mind to Consciousness, Dharana is the established conscious presence in Consciousness.

123. Remaining independent of everything as a result of the unassailable thought, "I am verily Brahman", is well known by the word Dhyana (meditation), and is productive of supreme bliss.

The highest happiness is when Dhyana (meditation) leads to conscious presence in Brahman.

124. The complete forgetfulness of all thought by first making it changeless and then identifying it with Brahman is called Samadhi known also as knowledge.

Thoughts and Samadhi are incompatible like fire and water. Therefore, all thought activity must be transcended in order for presence in Samadhi to be established. A sign that Samadhi is established is that the thoughts are erased.

125. The aspirant should carefully practice this (meditation) that reveals his natural bliss until, being under his full control, it arises spontaneously, in an instant when called into action.

When (meditation) the conscious presence becomes present in happiness, there also arises a need to express the happiness in action.

126. Then he, the best among Yogis having attained to perfection, becomes free from all practices. The real nature of such a man never becomes an object of the mind or speech.

The yogi who has established transcendence of mind does not need exercises in this.

127-128. While practicing Samadhi there appear unavoidably many obstacles, such as lack of inquiry, idleness, desire for sense-pleasure, sleep, dullness, distraction, tasting of joy, and the sense of blankness. One desiring the knowledge of Brahman should slowly get rid of such innumerable obstacles.

*Striving for Samadhi is not something to which the mind
is willing but resists, which can take various forms. These
obstacles must be removed.*

129. While thinking of an object the mind verily identifies
itself with that, and while thinking of a void it really becomes blank, whereas by the thought of Brahman it attains to
perfection. So one should constantly think of (Brahman to
attain) perfection.

*Constant presence in Brahman results in perfection and
liberation.*

130. Those who give up this supremely purifying thought
of Brahman, live in vain and are on the same level with
beasts.

*He who does not take advantage of the opportunity to be
present in Brahman misses the most important gift of life
and remains on the mundane level of the mind.*

131. Blessed indeed are those virtuous persons who at first
have this Consciousness of Brahman and then develop it
more and more. They are respected everywhere.

Some people are already established in Godconsciousness at birth and then during life develop a verbal and intellectual expression of this awareness. These people are considered wise by those around them.

132. Only those in whom this Consciousness (of Brahman) being ever present grows into maturity, attain to the state of ever-existent Brahman; and not others who merely deal with words.

Brahmanconsciousness is characterized by a presence in eternity and not an intellectual creation of words.

133. Also those persons who are only clever in discussing about Brahman but have no realization, and are very much attached to worldly pleasures, are born and die again and again in consequence of their ignorance. No one becomes present in Brahman through intellectual discussions. Only through spiritual maturity does one reach insight. It is not certain that one will reach this maturity in this life and future births are then required.

134. The aspirants after Brahman should not remain a single moment without the thought of Brahman, just like Brahma, Sanaka, Suka and others.

To be present in Brahman means to be consciously present in lifeenergy and being of total existence.

135. The nature of the cause inheres in the effect and not vice versa; so through reasoning it is found that in the absence of the effect, the cause, as such also disappears.

Often it is a desire for a certain effect that creates a cause. If this desire disappears, the cause also disappears.

136. Then that pure reality (Brahman) which is beyond speech alone remains. This should be understood again and again verily through the illustration of earth and the pot.

As cause and effect (karma) no longer affects, there remains pure reality (Consciousness) which is non-dualistic and beyond all change.

137. In this way alone there arises in the pure-minded a state of awareness (of Brahman), which is afterwards merged into Brahman.

There is only one state of consciousness; Godconsciousness or Brahman Consciousness. At the relative dualistic level there are a variety of levels of awareness. The one with pure heart and pure body and Soul can be present in God Consciousness – Brahman.

138. One should first look for the cause by the negative method and then find it by the positive method, as ever inherent in the effect.

The negative method refers to a non-dualistic non-attachment while the positive method refers to a dualistic attachment.

139. One should verily see the cause in the effect, and then dismiss the effect altogether. What then remains, the sage himself becomes.

If one is to be able to dismiss the effect, one must be independent of the cause. Only the sage who is present in Consciousness can have the right approach. If you have a normally developed nervous system, it goes without saying that you feel an influence in the nervous system, but the effect will vary depending on how bound you are to the influence.

140. A person who meditates upon a thing with great assiduity and firm conviction, becomes that very thing. This may be understood from the illustration of the wasp and the worm.

By focusing on the wasp, the worm may appear to eventually become a wasp.

141. The wise should always think with great care of the invisible, the visible, and everything else, as his own Self which is Consciousness itself.

Keeping existence and the Self in focus at the same time can make it easier to be consciously present in Consciousness.

142. Having reduced the visible to the invisible, the wise should think of the universe as one with Brahman. Thus alone will he abide in eternal felicity with mind full of awareness and bliss.

Realizing that everything is Brahman and the Self is Brahman (Aham Brahmasmi) gives a state of awareness filled with eternal happiness and bliss.

143. Thus has been described Raja-Yoga consisting of these steps (mentioned above). With this is to be combined Hatha-Yoga for (the benefit of) those whose worldly desires are partially attenuated.

144. For those whose mind is completely purified this (Raja-Yoga) alone is productive of perfection. Purity of the mind, again, is speedily accessible to those who are devoted to the teacher and the Deity.

Raja-Yoga is often referred to as the royal path to Yoga. It includes both meditation and various physical exercises that will purify body and mind to facilitate presence in Consciousness (Samadhi) and through God's grace establish permanent enlightenment.

Thus concludes Aparokshanubhutti – Self-realization.
Om shanti shanti shanti!

Bhaja Govindam

Worship of Govinda

by

Sri Adi Shankara

Shankaracharya

Translation & comments

Jan Fahleman

Preface

Adi Shankara through his wisdom has written and commented on many important Hindu works such as; The Upanishads, the Brahma Sutras and the Bhagavad-Gita. He was a representative of Advaita Vedanta, the non-dualistic philosophy. But he has also written works considered as Bhakti which describe devotion to God.

He was often traveling with his disciples in India. It is said that Bhaja Govindam came about when they saw an old man who was making an effort to learn Sanskrit and its grammar. Shankara thought it better that the old man spend his last years in devotion to God. Thereby he was inspired to write Bhaja Govindam. Bhaja Govindam can be recited but usually the verses are sung.

Sukta 1

bhaja govinda
bhaja govinda
govinda bhaja mūhamate
samprāpte sannihite kāle
nahi nahi rakśhati ukrikarae

Sukta 2

mūha jahīhi dhanāgamatśhā
kuru sadbuddhim manasi vitśhām
yallabhase nija karmopātta
vitta tena vinodaya chittam

Sukta 3

nārī stanabhara nābhīdeśa
dśhvā mā gā mohāveśam
etanmāsa vasādi vikāra
manasi vichintayā vāravāram

Sukta 1
Worship Govinda,
Worship Govinda,
Worship Govinda.
Oh fool! Rules of Grammar
will not save you at the time of your death.

Sukta 2
O fool!
Give up your thirst to amass wealth,
devote your mind to dispassion
and thoughts of the Real.
Be content with what comes to you through actions
performed by your own work.

Sukta 3
Do not get drowned in delusion,
infatuated with passion and lusty desires,
by seeing a woman's raised breasts and navel.
These are nothing but a modification of flesh and fat,
and the like. Do not fail to remember this again
and again in your mind.

Sukta 4

nainī daagata jalamati taraa
tadvajjīvita matiśaya chapalaṁ |
viddhi vyādhyabhimāna grasta
loka śokahata cha samastam

Sukta 5

yāvad-vittopārjana sakta
tāvan-nijaparivāro rakta
paśchājjīvati jarjara dehe
vārtā koapi na pcChati gehe

Sukta 6

yāvat-pavano nivasati dehe
tāvat-pchChati kuśalagehe |
gatavati vāyau dehāpāye
bhāryā bibhyati tasmin kāye

Sukta 4

*As water drops on a lotus leaf
are unsteady and trembling,
in the same way life in this world
is exceedingly unsteady and restless.
Know that the whole world is full of miseries,
afflicted by unhappiness and grief.*

Sukta 5

*So long as a man is fit and able to support his family by
earning wealth, all those family members around him
show affection. But no one at home cares for him, even
have a word with him, when his body becomes invalid and
totters due to old age.*

Sukta 6

*When one is alive, his family members enquire kindly
about his welfare. But when the life-air stops and the soul
departs from the body, even his wife runs away in fear of the
corpse.*

Sukta 7

bāla stāvat krīāsakta

tarua stāvat taruīsakta

vddha stāvat-chintāmagna

parame brahmai koapi na lagna

Sukta 8

kā te kāntā kaste putra

sasāroayamatīva vichitra

kasya tva vā kuta āyāta

tatva chintaya tadiha bhrāta

Sukta 9

satsagatve nissagatva

nissagatve nirmohatvam

nirmohatve niśchalatattva

niśchalatattve jīvanmukti

Sukta 7

Childhood is lost in attachment to games.
The youth is lost in attachment to woman.
Old age passes with worry and anxiety,
thinking over many things.
But there is hardly anyone who wants to be
lost (attached) in Para-Brahman, the Supreme Spirit.

Sukta 8

Who is your wife? Who is your son?
Supremely wonderful is samsāra,
the circle of birth and death.
Of whom are you?
From where have you come?
Brother, ponder over these concepts.

Sukta 9

Being in the company of good people (saints)
gives rise to non-attachment;
from non-attachment comes freedom from delusion,
which leads to awareness of reality;
understanding of reality gives rise to emancipation
leading to the liberation of the soul
(jīvan-mukti), while still alive.

Sukta 10

vayasi gate ka kāmavikāra
śuśhke nīre kakāsāra
kśhīe vitte ka parivāra
GYāte tattve ka sasāra

Sukta 11

mā kuru dhanajana yauvana garva
harati nimeśhāt-kāla sarvam
māyāmayamidam-akhila hitvā
brahmapada tva praviśa viditvā

Sukta 12

dina yāminyau sāya prāta
śiśira vasantau punarāyāta
kāla krīati gacChatyāyu
tadapi na muñchatyāśāvāyu

Sukta 10

What good is lust when youth has fled?
What use is a lake which has no water?
Where are the relatives when wealth is gone?
What is samsāra(transmigratory process),
when Truth is known.

Sukta 11

Do not take pride in wealth,
friends and youth.
Each one of these is destroyed within an instant by Time.
Free yourself from the illusion of the world of māyā
and attain the realm of Brahman, timeless truth.

Sukta 12

Day and night, evening and morning,
winter and summer come and go again and again.
Eternal time plays and life ebbs away,
yet one does not let go of the storm of desire.

Sukta 13

dvādaśa mañjarikābhira śeśha
kathito vaiyā karaasyaiśha
upadeśo bhūd-vidyā nipuai
śrīmacChakara bhagavacCharaai

Sukta 14

kā te kāntā dhana gata chintā
vātula ki tava nāsti niyantā
trijagati sajjana sagatirekā
bhavati bhavārava tarae naukā

Sukta 15

jailo muī luñjita keśa
kāśhāyānbara bahukta veśha
paśyannapi cha na paśyati mūha
udara nimitta bahukta veśha

Sukta 13
The bouquet of twelve verses
was imparted to a grammarian
by the all-knowing Śankara,
adored as Bhagavat-pāda.

Sukta 14
O, mad man!
Why this engrossment in thoughts
of wealth and beloved?
Is there no one to guide you?
In these thee worlds,
only the association with saintly people (satsanga)
can serve as the boat that can steer cross the ocean of
repeated birth and death.
(Stanza attributed to Padmapāda.)

Sukta 15
There are many (ascetics) with matted hair,
many with clean shaven heads,
many whose hair have been plucked out;
some are clothed in orange,
yet others parading in various colors -
Indeed, these different disguises or apparels
are only for their belly's sake.
Seeing the truth revealed before them,
still the foolish ones can not see through these many
disguises. (Stanza attributed to Totakācārya.)

Sukta 16

aga galita palita mua
daśana vihīna jāta tuam
vddho yāti ghītvā daa
tadapi na muñchatyāśā piam

Sukta 17

agre vahni pśhhe bhānu
rātrau chubuka samarpita jānu
karatala bhikśhas-tarutala vāsa
tadapi na muñchatyāśā pāśa

Sukta 18

kurute gagā sāgara gamana
vrata paripālanam-athavā dānam
GYāna vihīna sarvamatena
bhajati na mukti janma śatena

Sukta 16
Strength has left the old man's body;
his head has become bald,
his gums toothless and leaning on crutches.
Even then he can not let go of his attachment,
clinging firmly to fruitless hopes and desires.
(Stanza attributed to Hastamalaka.)

Sukta 17
The ascetic warms his body with fire
in front and the sun at the back.
At night he dwells under a tree
with face huddled between the knees
to keep out of the cold.
In his hands he holds the beggar's alms
and yet he does not let go of the noose
of attachment to desire and passion.
(Stanza attributed to Subhodha.)

Sukta 18
One may travel (on a pilgrimage)
to the confluence where the Gangā
river meets the ocean (gangā-sāgara),
undertake vows and give away in charity,
however without true knowledge (jñāna)
one will not achieve liberation (mukti)
even in a hundred lifetimes,
according to all [schools of] thought. (Stanza attributed to
Vārtikakāra.)

Sukta 19

suramandira taru mūla nivāsa
śayyā bhūtalam-ajina vāsa
sarva parigraha bhogatyāga
kasya sukha na karoti virāga

Sukta 20

yogarato vā bhogarato vā
sagarato vā sagavihīna
yasya brahmai ramate chitta
nandati nandati nandatyeva

Sukta 21

bhagavadgītā kiñchidadhītā
gangā jalalava kaikā pītā
sakdapi yena murārī samarchā
kriyate tasya yamena na charchā

Sukta 19
One who lives in temples
or dwells at the foot of trees,
whose bed is the surface of the earth,
whose garment is a deer-skin,
who has thus renounced all enjoyment
of worldly possessions
– to whom will such dispassion (vairāgya) not bring
happiness?
(Stanza attributed to Nityānanda.)

Sukta 20
One may take delight in yoga (union with god)
or bhoga (worldly enjoyment);
may be delighted by company or solitude;
but he whose mind delights in brahman (the spiritual
truth), only he enjoys real bliss and is satisfied,
no one else.
(Stanza attributed to ānandagirih)

Sukta 21
Let a man read but a little from Bhagavad-gītā,
drink just a drop of Gangā-water,
worship but once murāri,
the enemy of 'Murā' (Lord Krsna);
he then will have no confrontation with Yama,
the Lord of death.
(Stanza attributed to Drdhabhakta.)

Sukta 22

punarapi janana punarapi maraa

punarapi jananī jahare śayanam

iha sasāre bahu dustāre

kpayā'pāre pāhi murāre

Sukta 23

rathyā charpaa virachita kantha

puyāpuya vivarjita pantha

yogī yoga niyojita chitta

ramate bālonmattavadeva

Sukta 24

kastva koaha kuta āyāta

kā me jananī ko me tāta

iti paribhāvaya nija sasāra

sarva tyaktvā svapna vichāram

Sukta 22
Birth again, death again,
again resting in the mother's womb!
It is indeed hard to cross this boundless ocean of
samsāra (cycle of repeated birth and death).
O Murāri! by your causeless mercy please
protect me (from this transmigratory process).
(Stanza attributed to Nityanātha.)

Sukta 23
The one whose patched garment
is made from tattered rags cast on the road,
whose path is free from sins having abandoned
virtue and vices, whose mind is fixed on
yoga (in union with god),
that yogi indeed rejoices (in divine bliss)
like a crazed wild child overwhelmed by happiness.
(Stanza attributed to Nityanātha.)

Sukta 24
Having abandoned this world,
knowing it to be without essence,
comparable to the reflection of a dream,
consider well and reflect: Who am I?
Who are you? Where have I come from?
Who is my mother, and who is my father?
(Stanza attributed to Surendra.)

Sukta 25

tvayi mayi sarvatraiko viśhu
vyartha kupyasi mayyasahiśhu
bhava samachitta sarvatra tva
vāñChasyachirād-yadi viśhutvam

Sukta 26

śatrau mitre putre bandhau
mā kuru yatna vigraha sandhau
sarvasminnapi paśyātmāna
sarvatrot-sja bhedāgyānam

Sukta 27

kāma krodha lobha moha
tyaktvā"tmāna paśyati soaham
ātmagynāna vihīnā mūhā
te pachyante naraka nigūhā

Sukta 25

In me, in you and in everything else,
none but the same (All-Pervading) Lord Visnu dwells.
Your anger and impatience is meaningless.
If you wish to attain the Supreme Visnu soon, be equalmin-
ded in all circumstances, have samabhāva,
equanimity, always.
(Stanza attributed to Medhātithira.)

Sukta 26

Do not waste your efforts to win the love
of or to fight against friend and foe,
children and relatives.
See the true self in everyone
and give up all feelings of duality completely.
(Stanza attributed to Medhātithira.)

Sukta 27

Give up lust, anger, greed and infatuation,
try to know the true self and consider:
Who am I?
Those fools covered by ignorance,
who lack self-knowledge (ātma-jñāna)
are tormented in hells.
(Stanza attributed to Bhārativamśa.)

Sukta 28

geya gītā nāma sahasra

dhyeya śrīpati rūpam-ajasram

neya sajjana sage chitta

deya dīnajanāya cha vittam

Sukta 29

sukhata kriyate rāmābhoga

paśchāddhanta śarīre roga

yadyapi loke maraa śaraa

tadapi na muñchati pāpācharaam

Sukta 30

arthamanartha bhāvaya nitya

nāsti tata sukha leśa satyam

putrādapi dhanabhājā bhīti

sarvatraiśhā vihitā rīti

Sukta 28

Regularly recite from the Gītā,
meditate on Visnu (śrīpati) in your heart,
and chant his thousand glories names (visnusahasranāma).
Take delight to be with the noble and the holy.
Distribute your wealth in charity to the poor and the needy.
(Stanza attributed to Sumatir.)

Sukta 29

Very readily one indulges in carnal pleasures
but later on, alas, come diseases of the body.
Even though in the world the ultimate end
is death (maranam),
even then one does not relinquish his sinful behaviours.

Sukta 30

Remember always that wealth
is the source of misfortune.
The truth is that one cannot extract
even a bit of happiness from it.
For the rich, there is fear even from one's own son.
This is the established way with wealth everywhere.

Sukta 31

prāāyāma pratyāhāra

nityānitya viveka vichāram

jāpyasameta samādhi vidhāna

kurva vadhāna mahad-avadhānam

Sukta 32

guru charaāmbhuja nirbharabhakta

sasārād-achirād-bhava mukta

sendiya mānasa niyamādeva

drakśhyasi nija hdayastha devam

Sukta 33

mūha kaśchina vaiyākarao

ukkaraādhyayana dhurīa

śrīmacChakara bhagavachchiśhyai

bodhita āsīcChodita karaai

Iti mohamudgara sapūra.

Om shanti shanti shanti!

Sukta 31

Practice control of breath (prānā-yāma)
and withdrawal of the senses
from their respective sense objects (pratyāhāra);
deliberate on the distinction between the
permanent and the transitory;
perform meditation along with
chanting the holy names of god;
perform these with great attention and extreme care!

Sukta 32

Oh devotee sincerely dedicated to
the lotus feet of the Guru!
May thou be soon free from Samsārā,
the circle of birth and death.
Through disciplined senses and controlled mind,
thou shalt come to see (experience)
the in-dwelling Lord of your heart.

Sukta 33

Thus a foolish grammarian lost in grammatical rules,
was cleansed of his narrow vision
and shown the light by the students
of the illustrious Śrīmad Śankarācārya.
Thus ends the Moha Mudgara (Hammer of Delusion –
Another name for Bhaja Govindam).
Om shanti shanti shanti!